This Book Belongs To:...

....

....

....

COLOR TEST PAGE

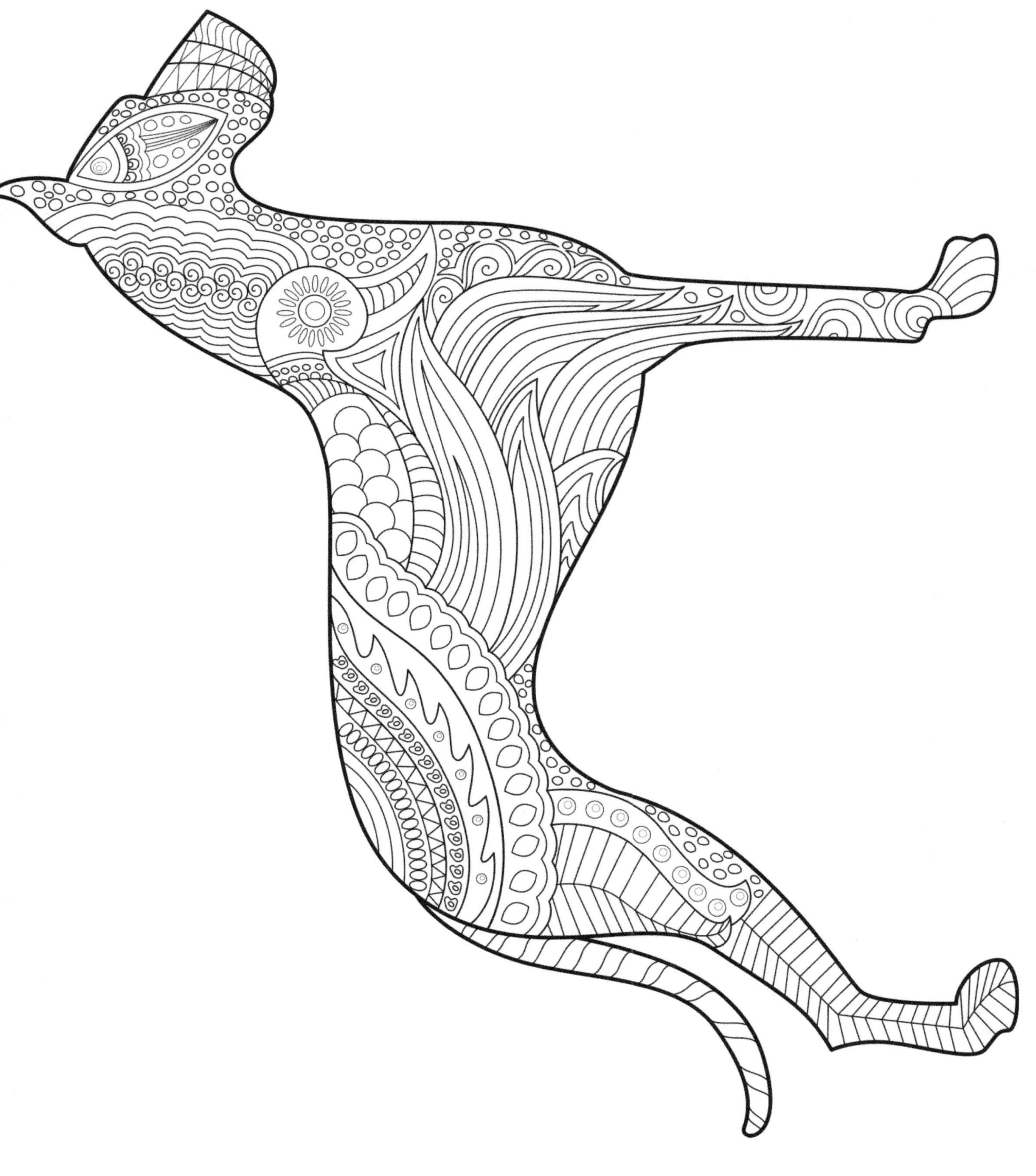

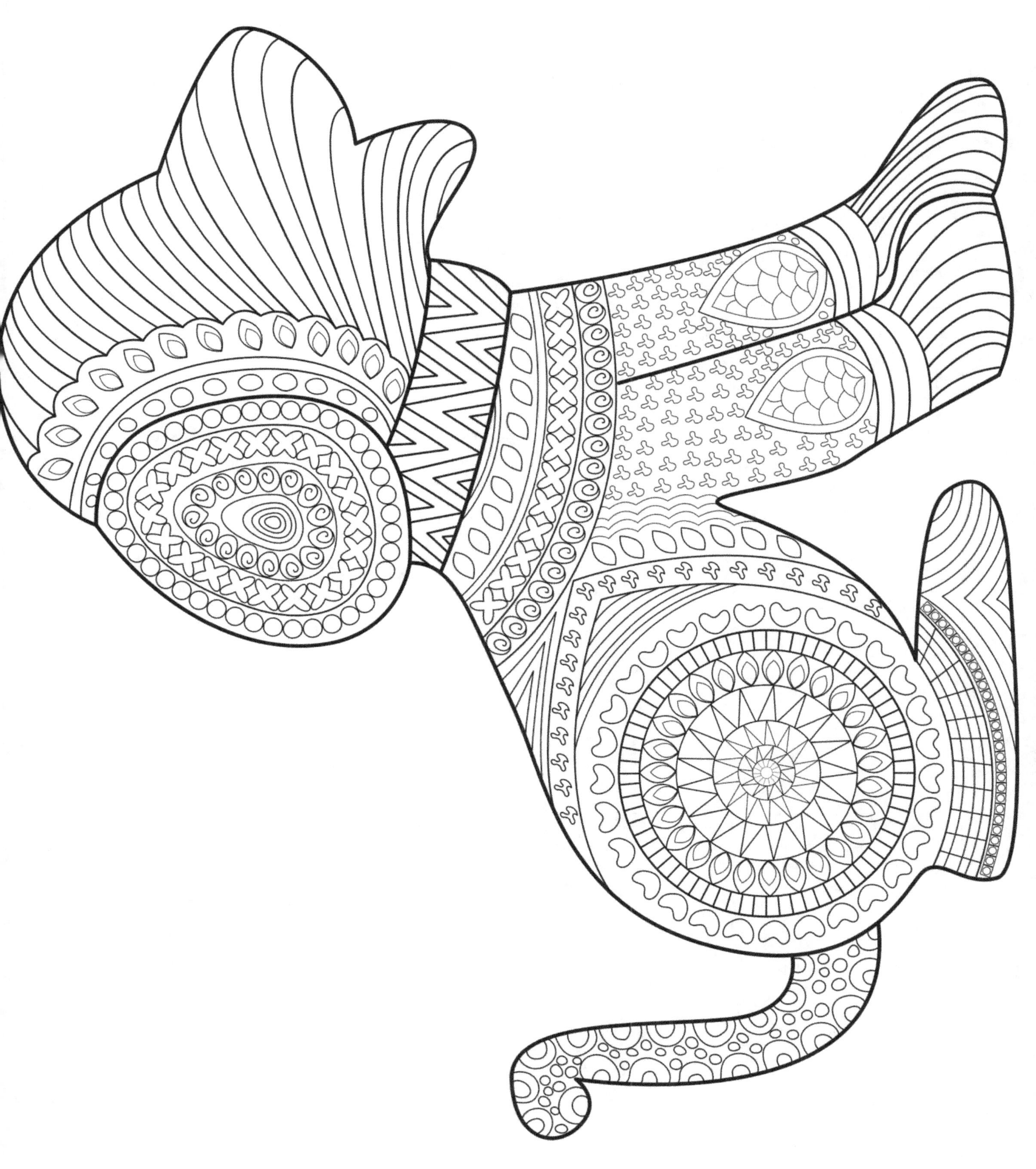

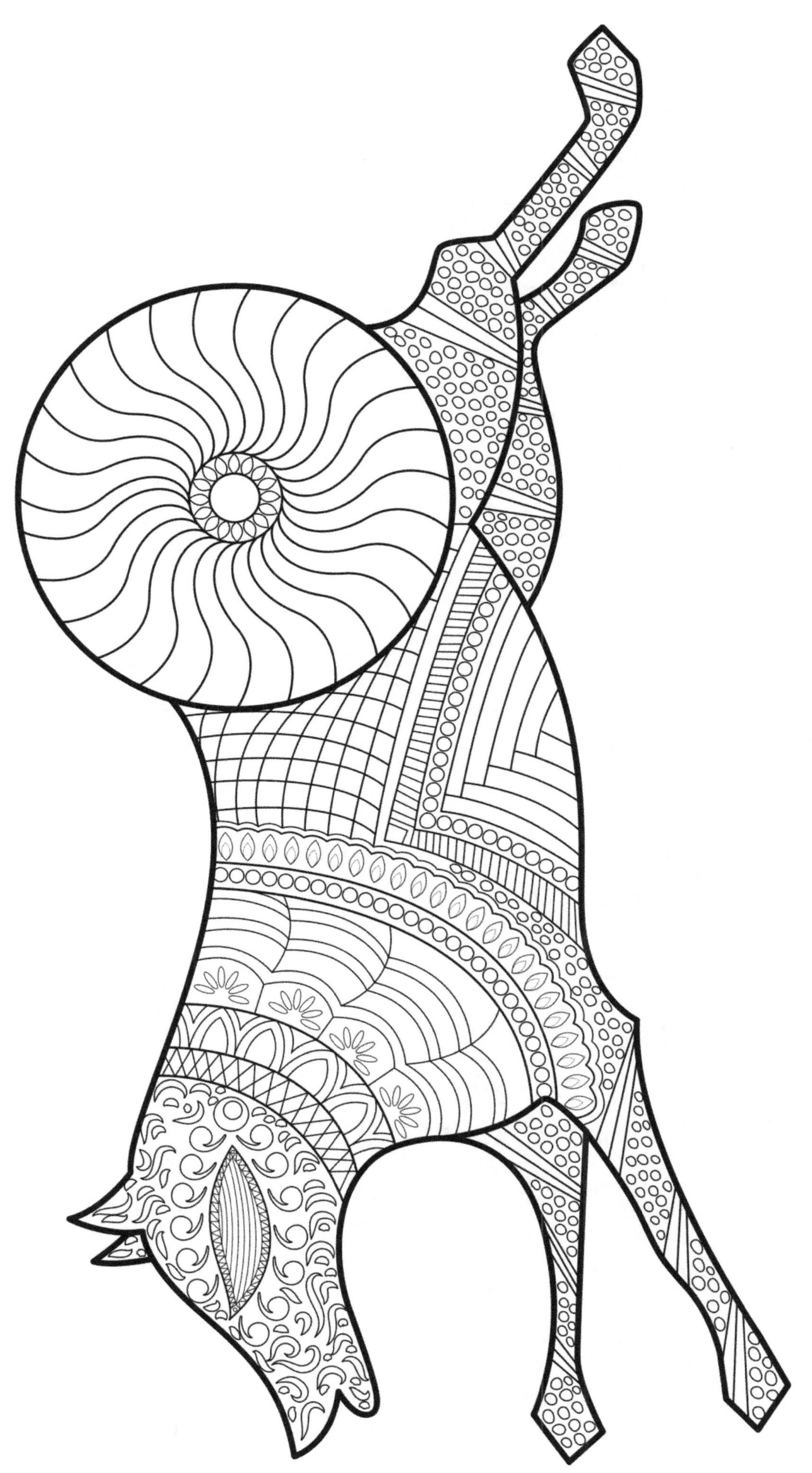

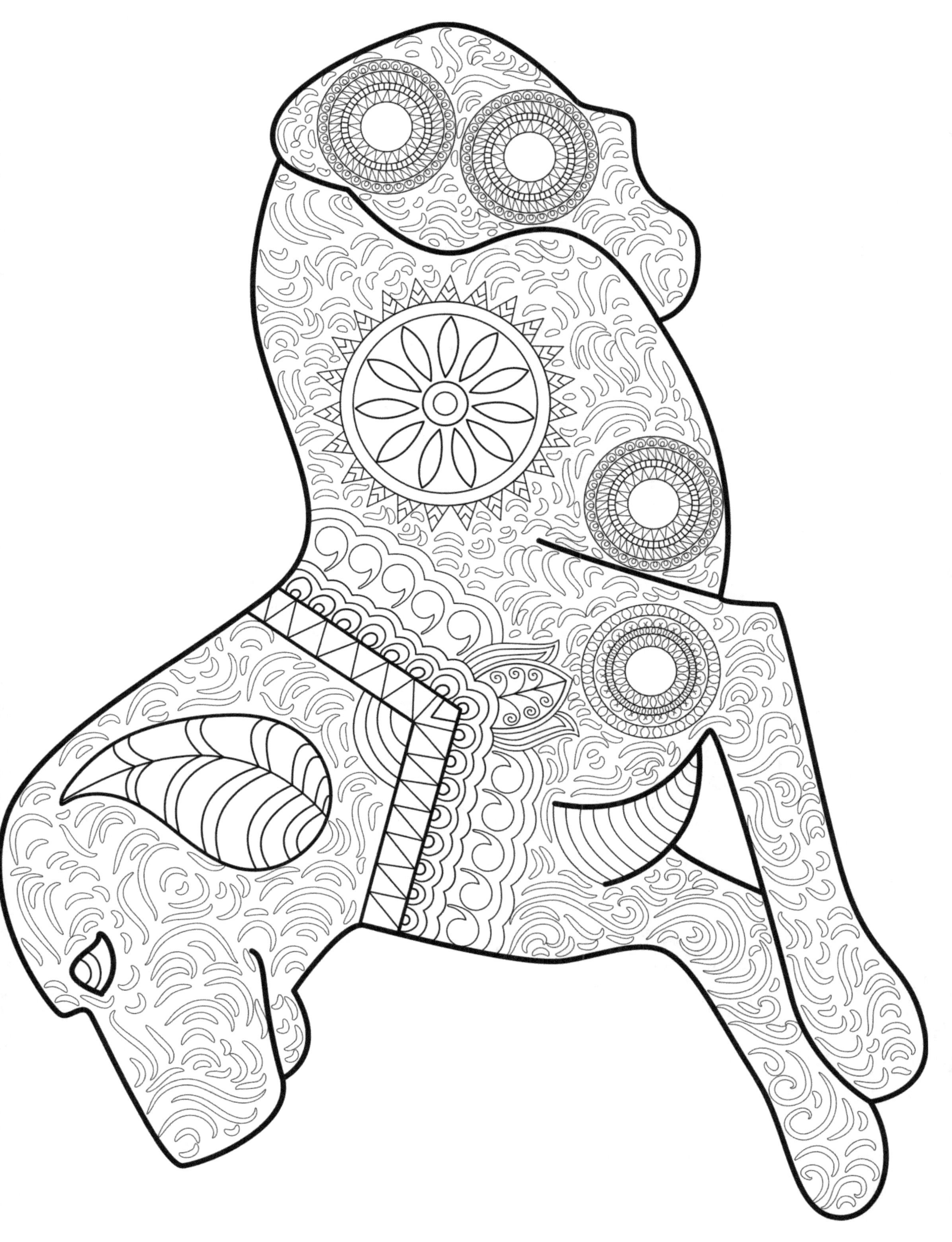

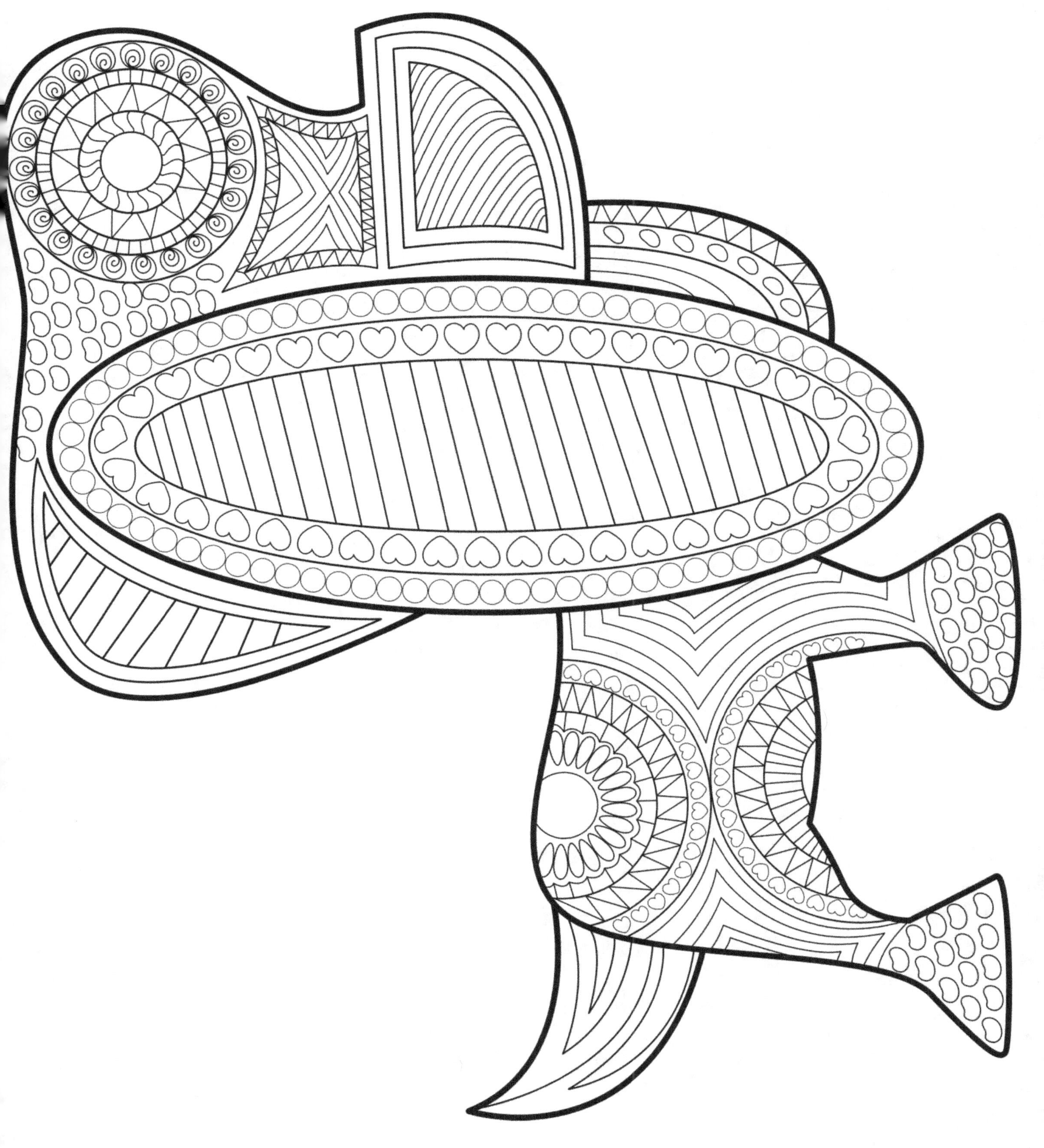

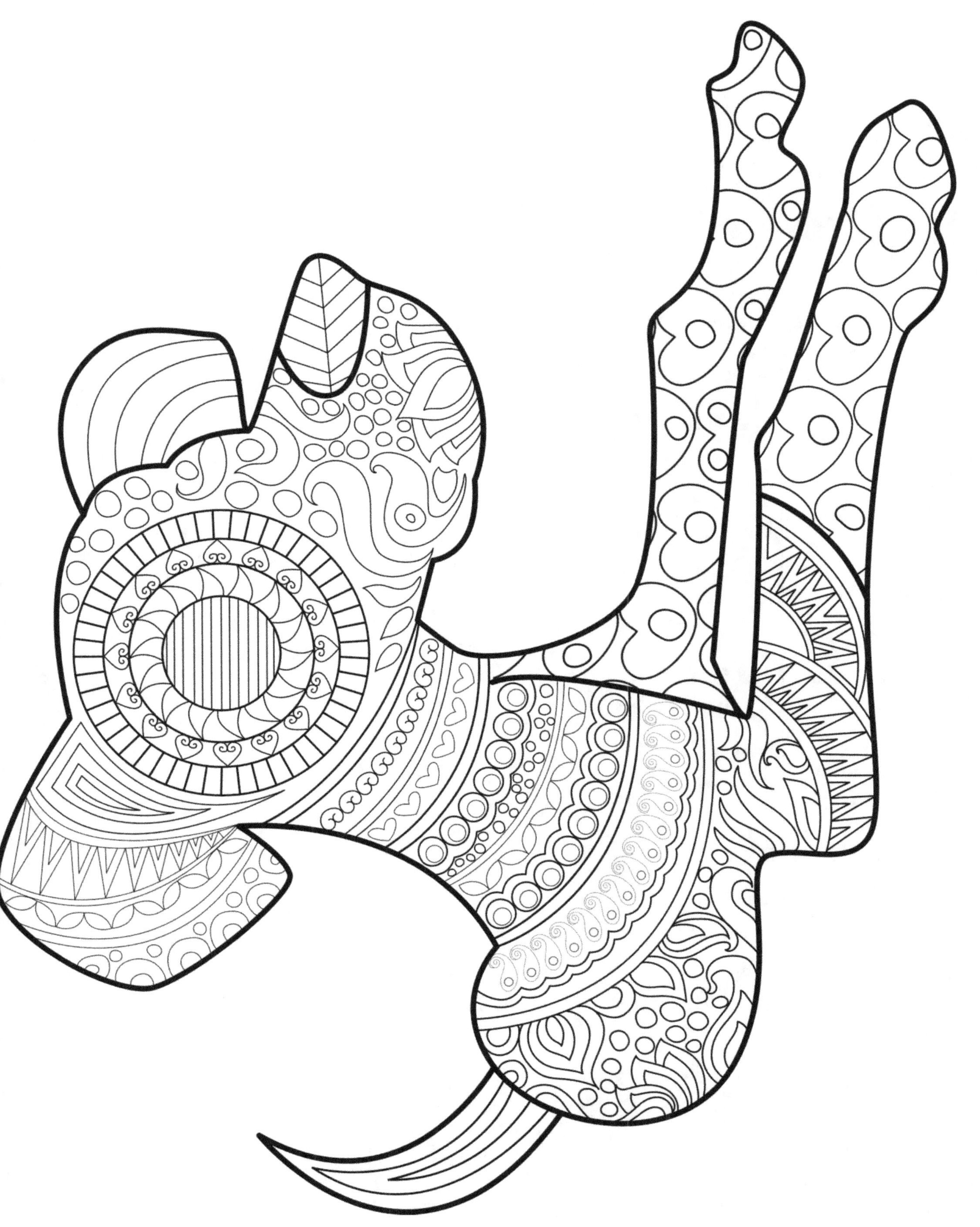

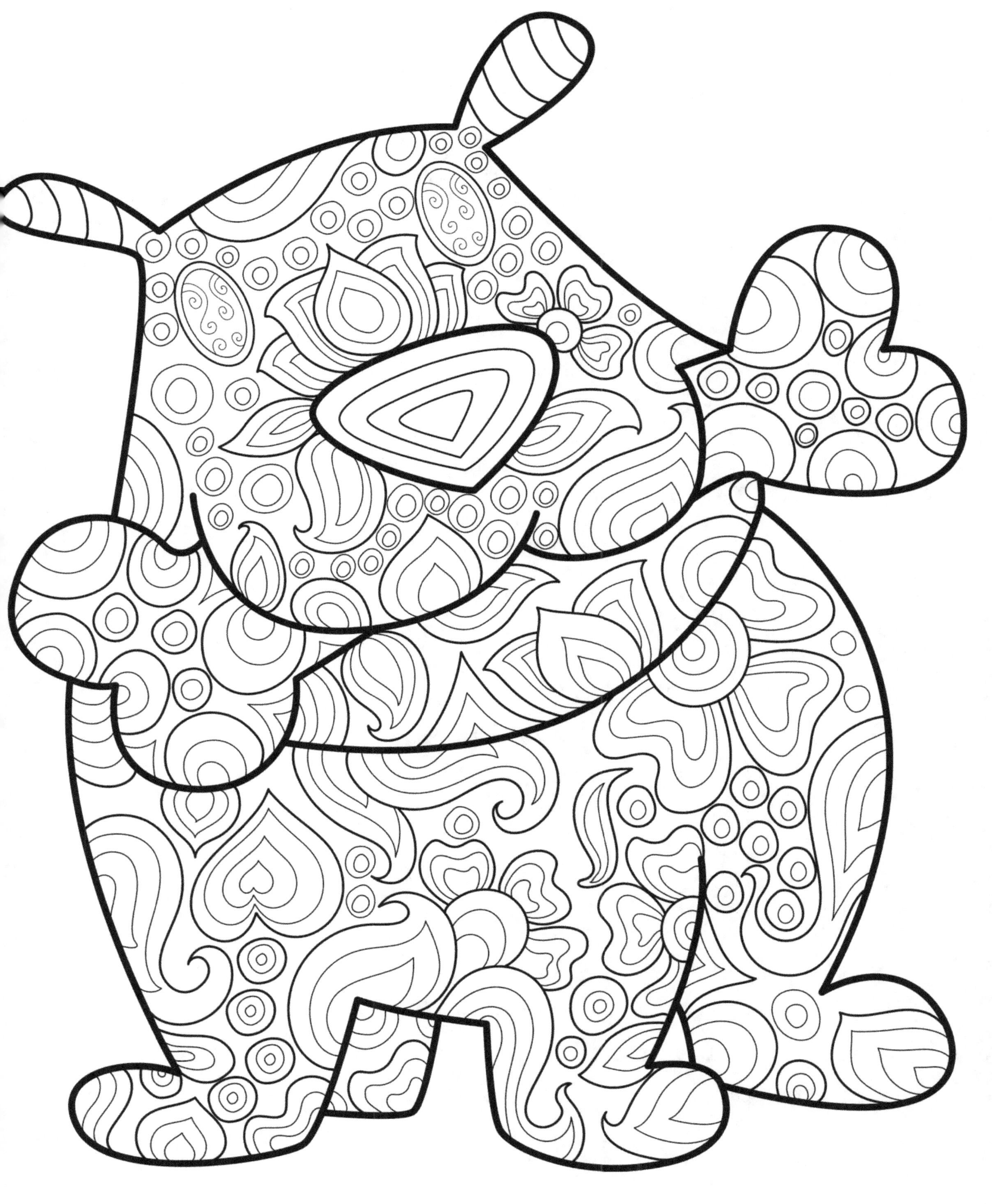

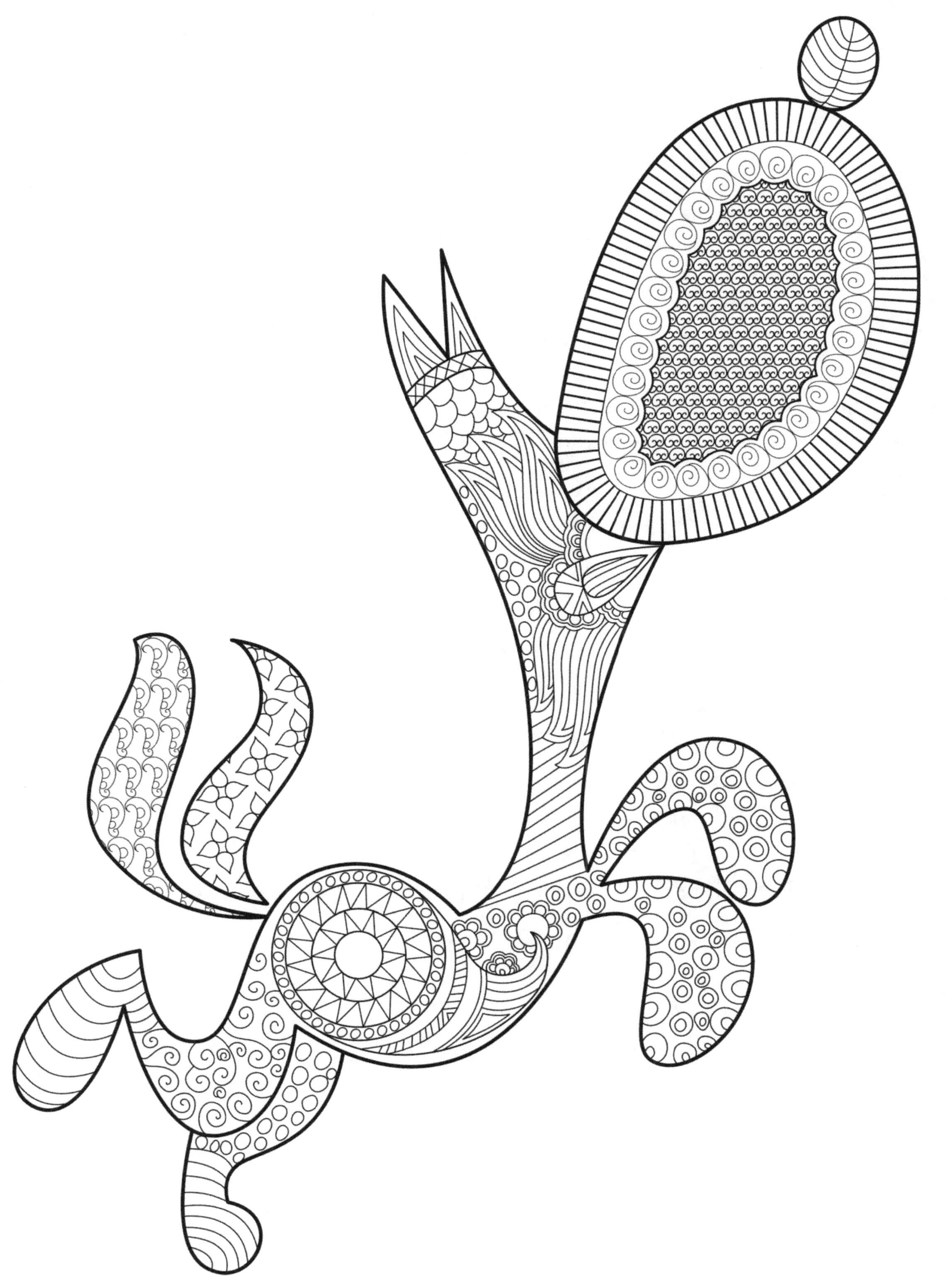

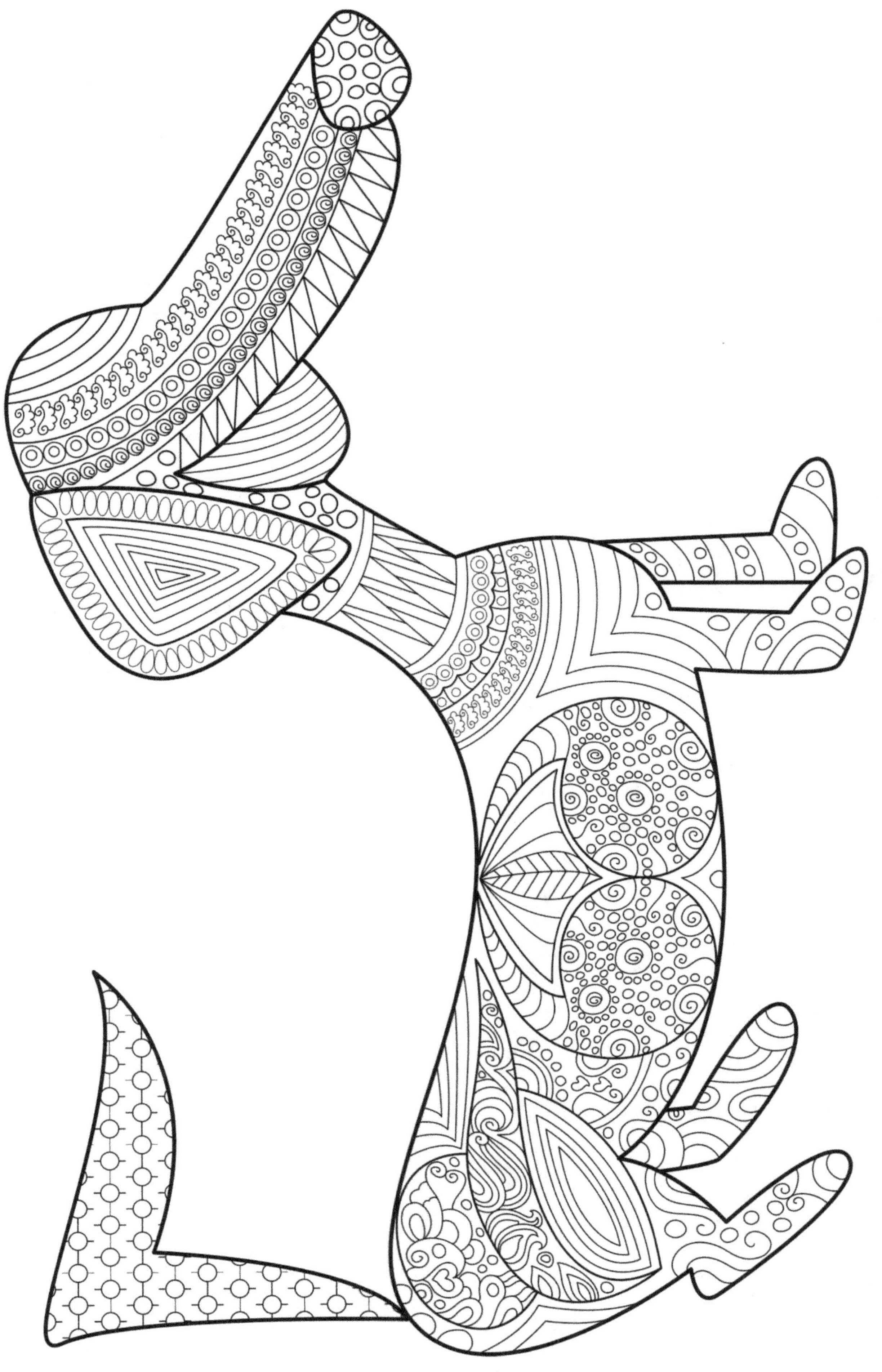

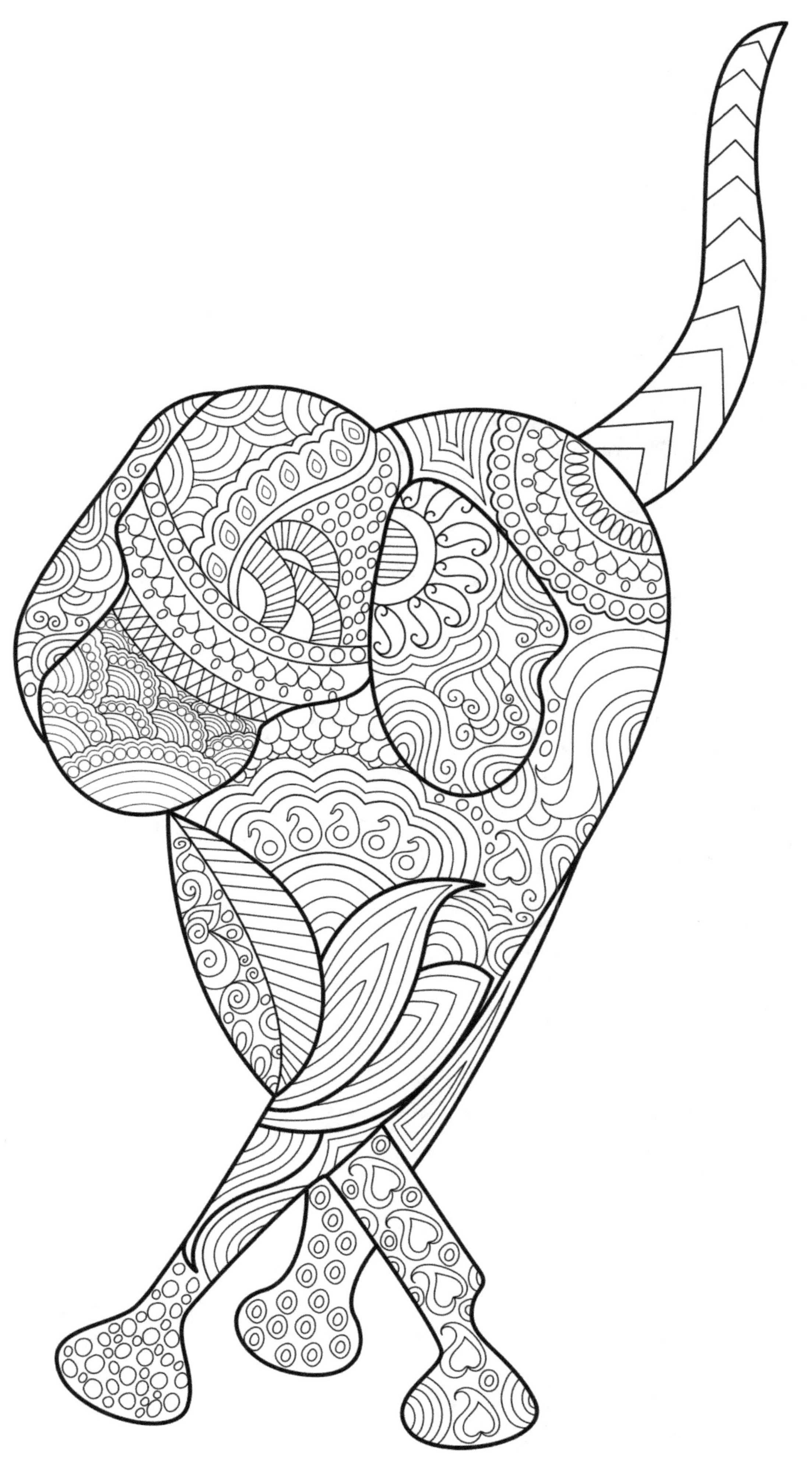

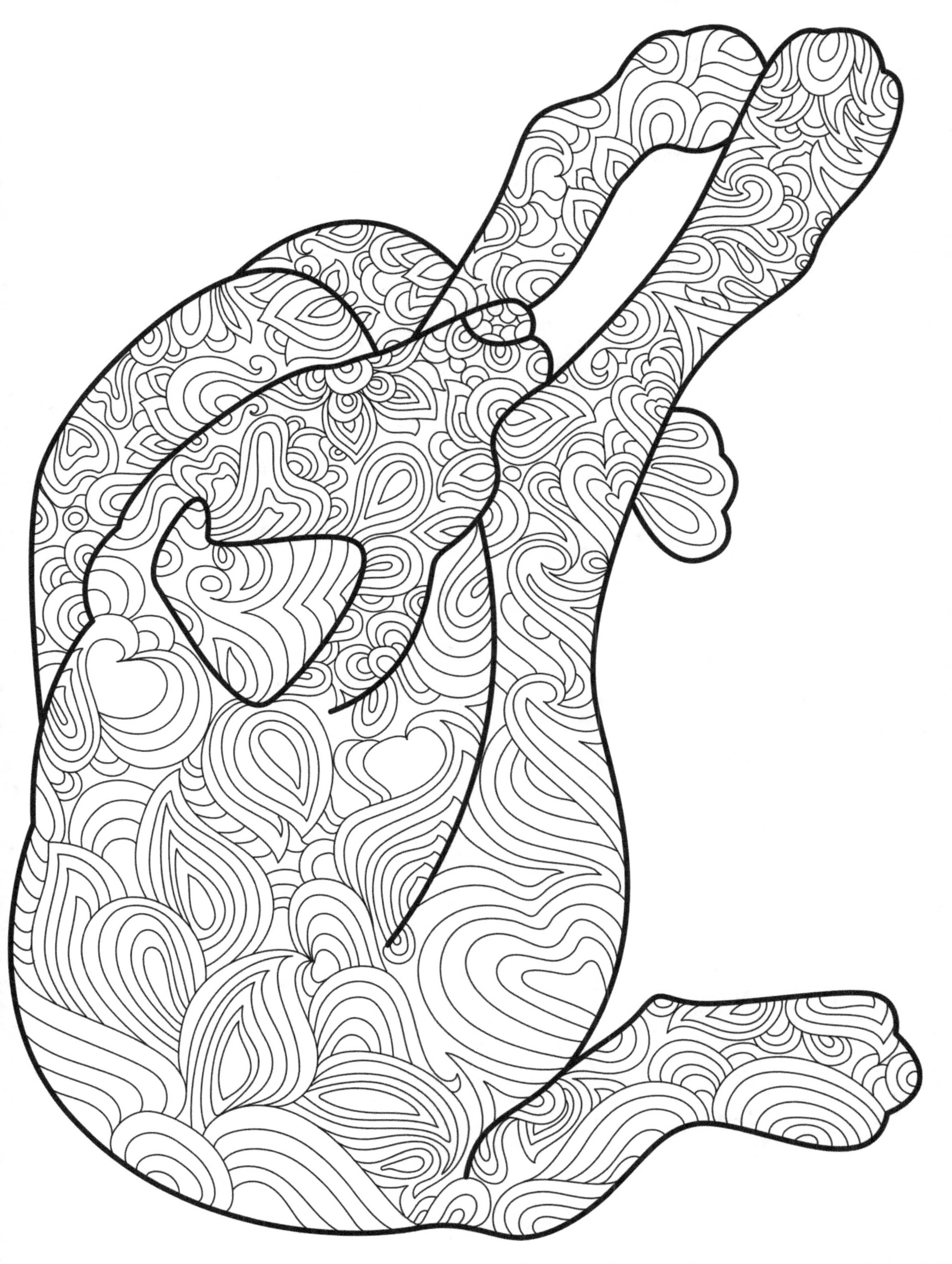

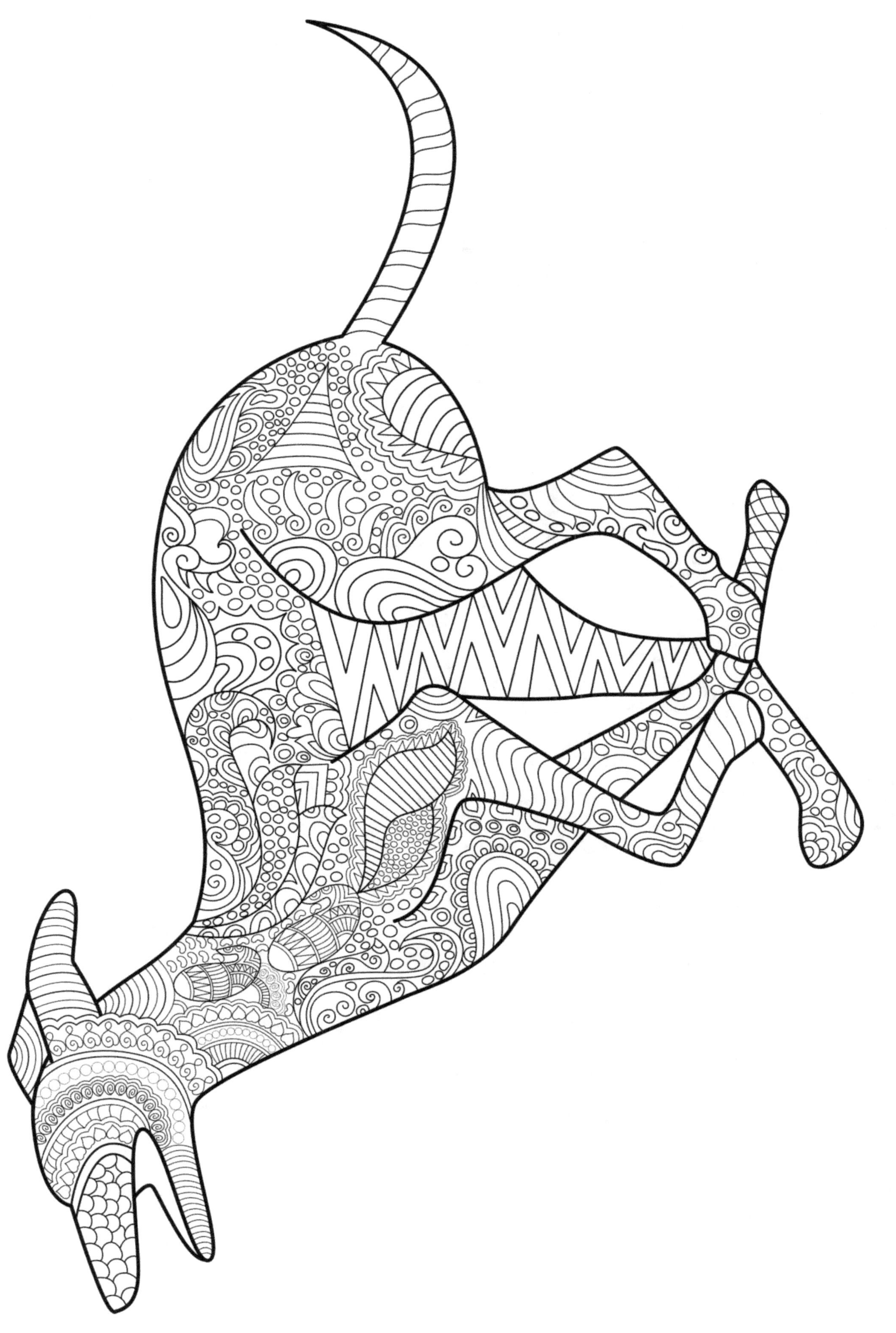

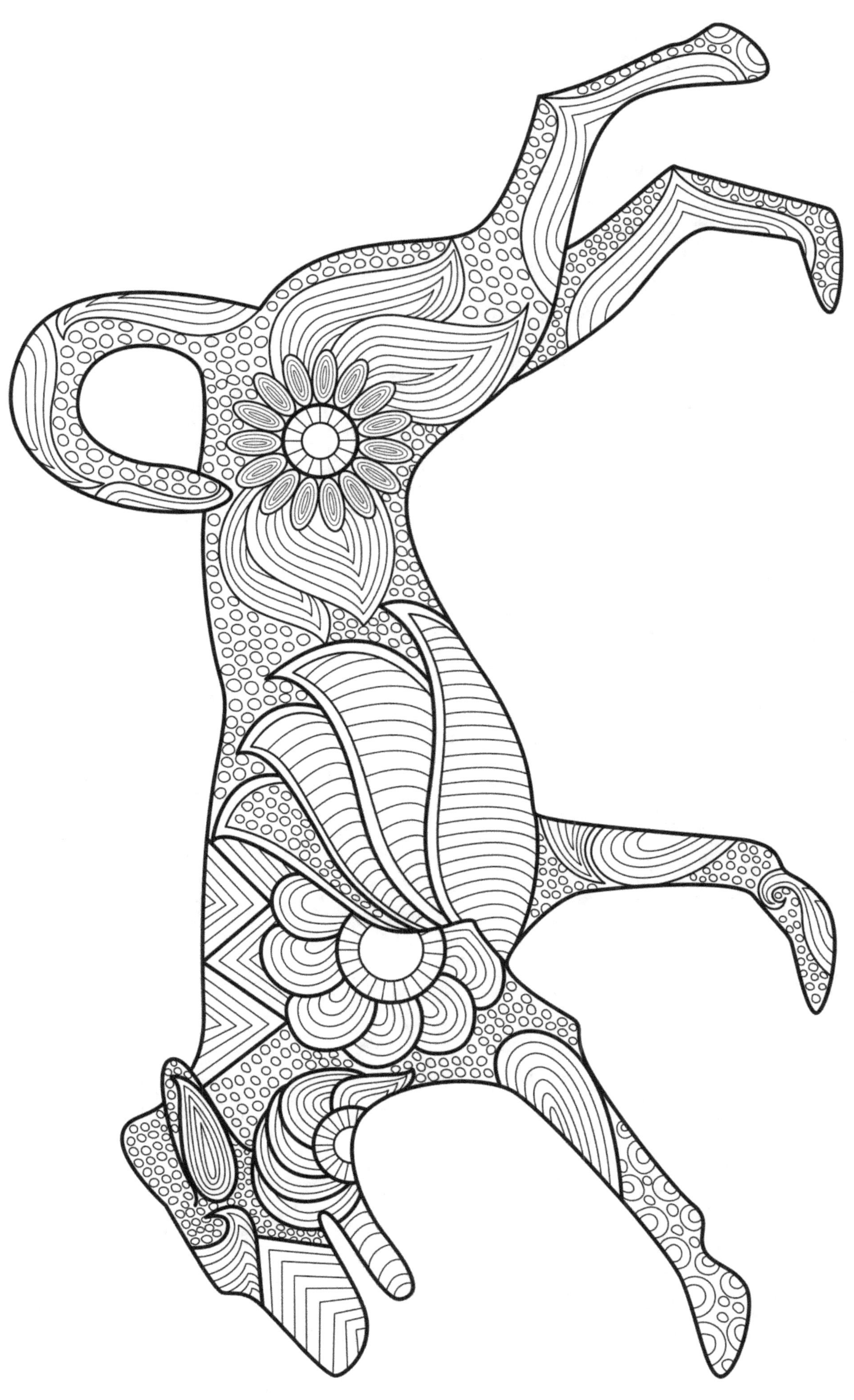

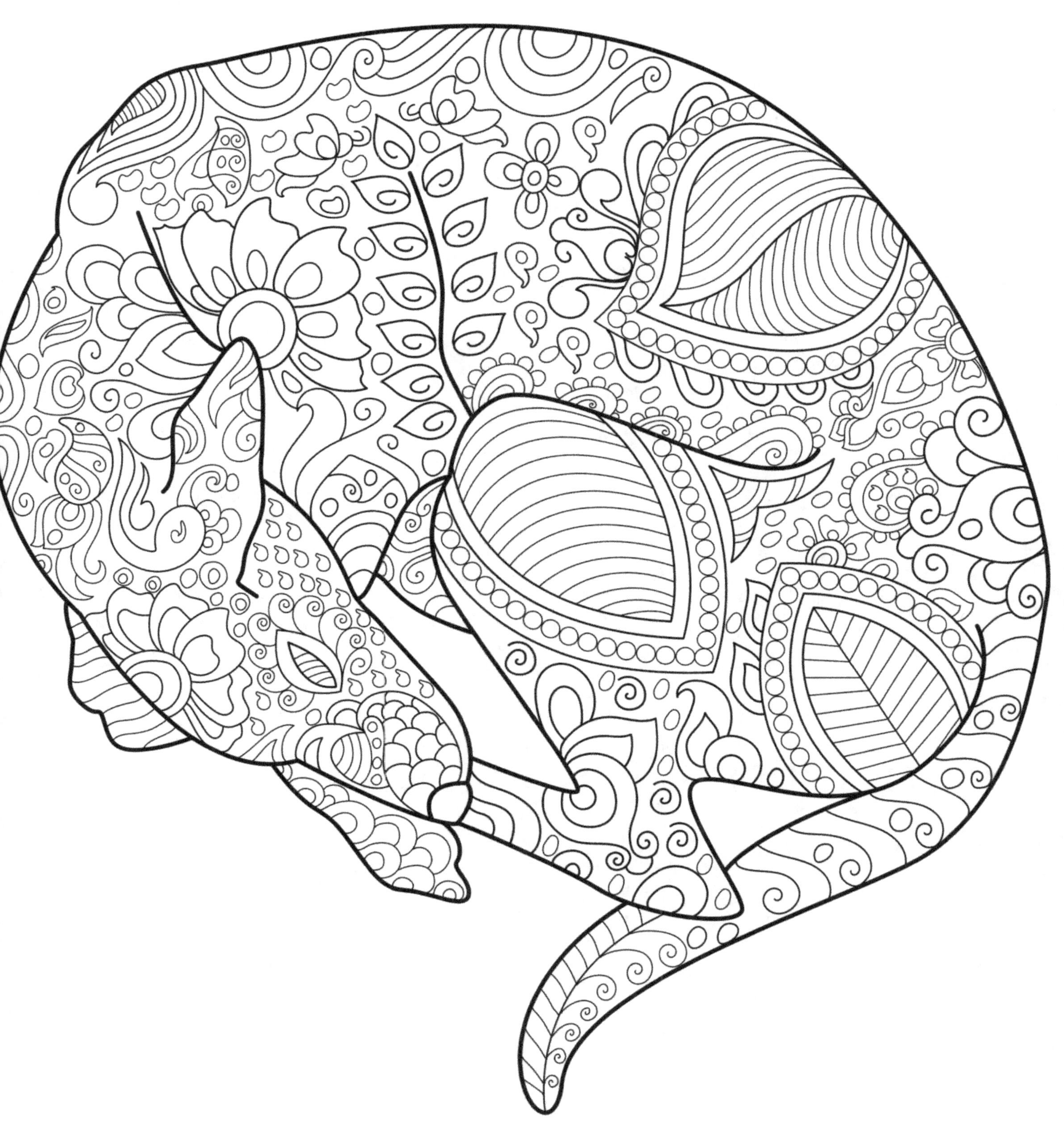

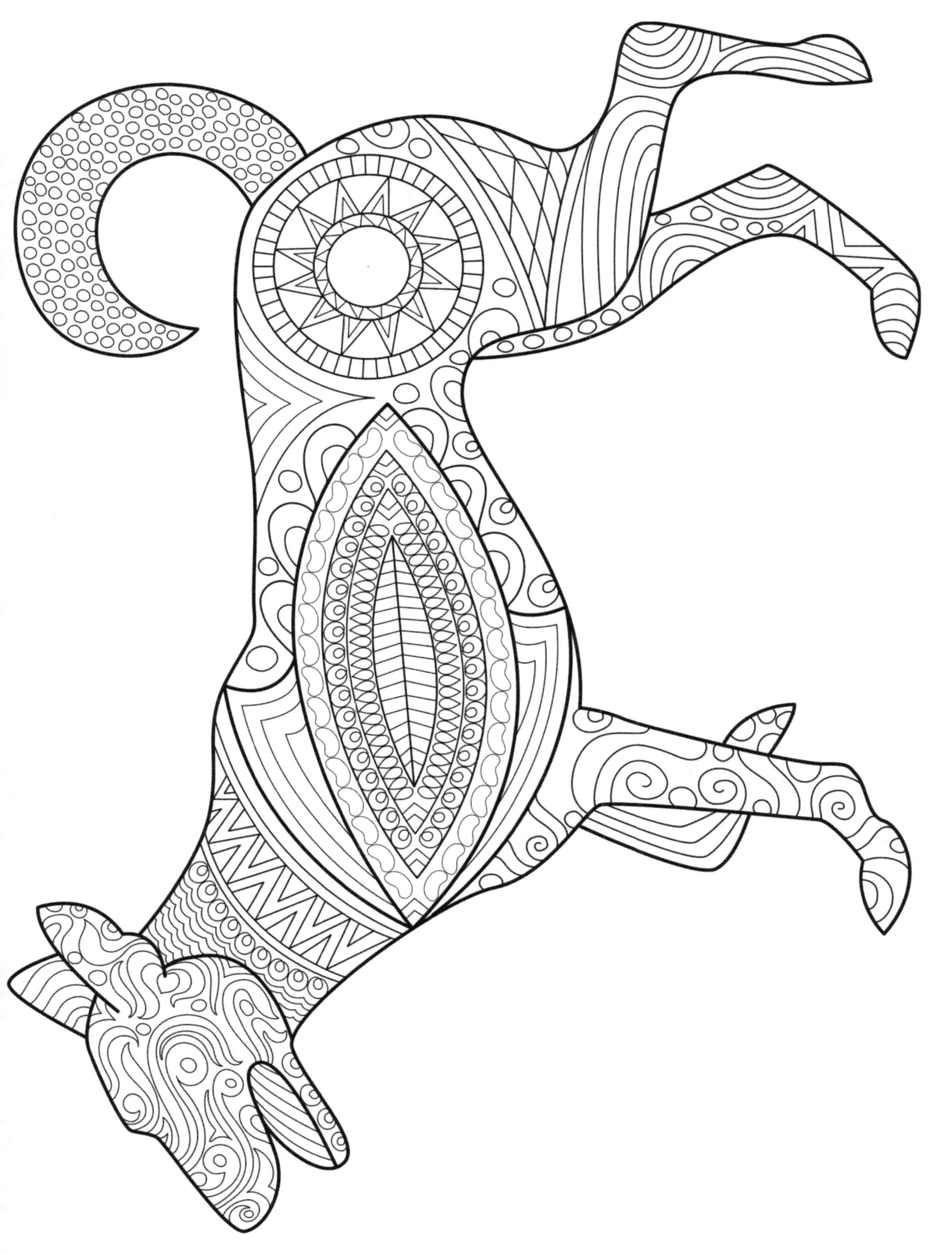

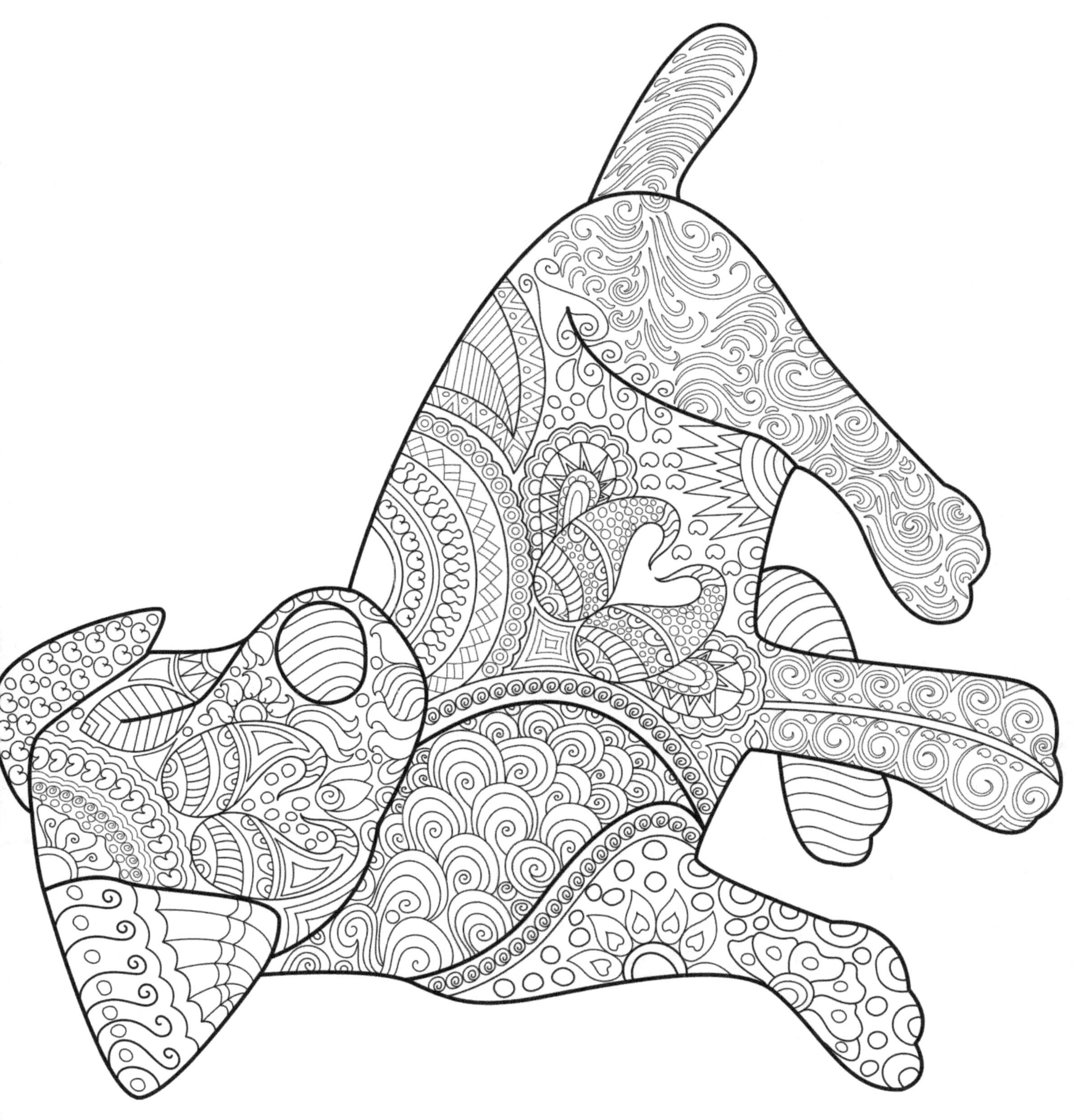

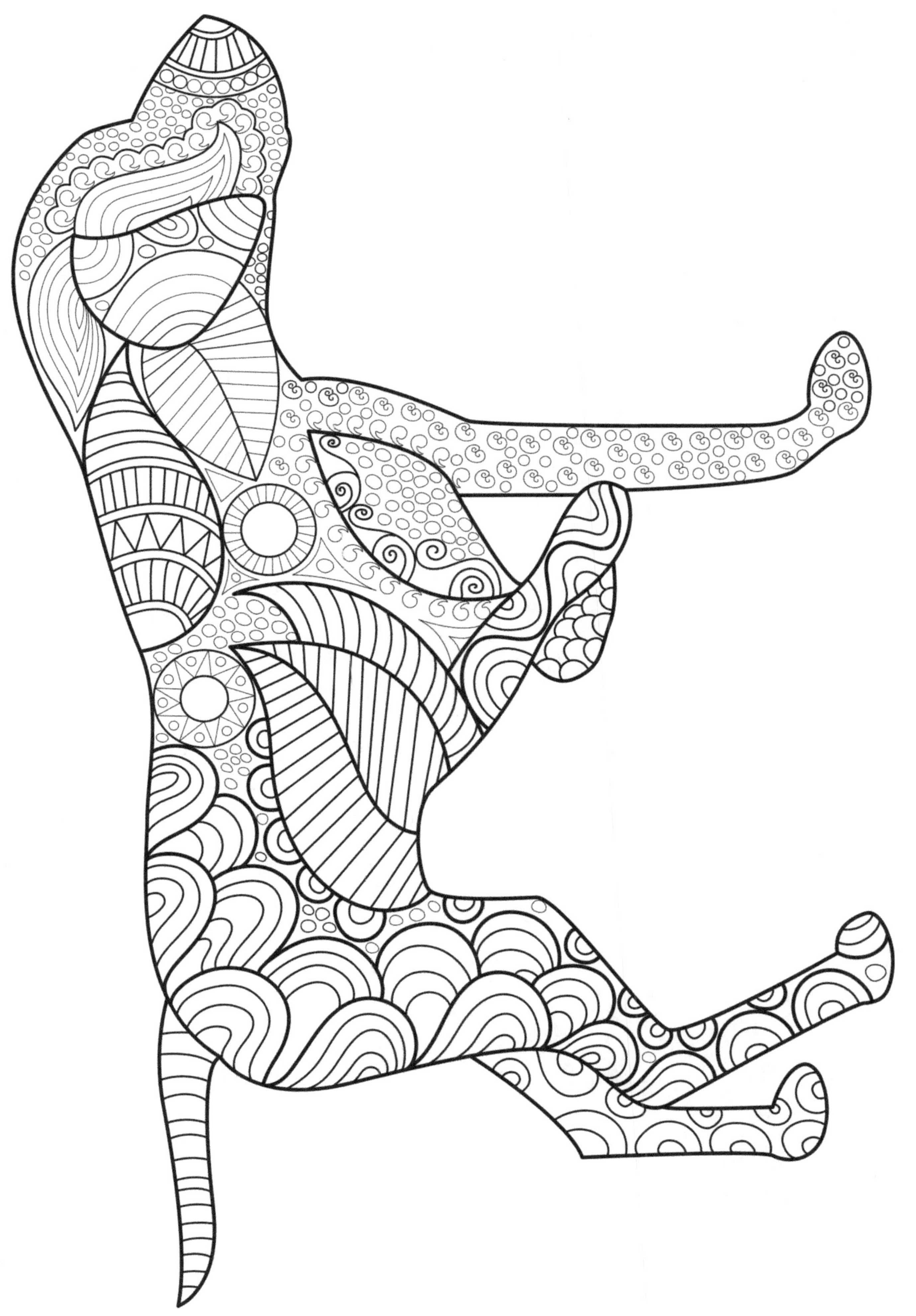

WE HOPE YOU ENJOYED THIS COLORING BOOK,
YOU CAN FIND MORE BOOKS ON OUR STORE.

Your Memories With This Book:

www.ingramcontent.com/pod-product-compliance
Lightning Source LLC
Chambersburg PA
CBHW081744250726
48657CB00010B/3400